# Contents

# CHAPTER ONE
## What I s  a Chihuahua?

Ever since the first Chihuahua made his American debut, he's become one popular little Chi muffin. With so much hoopla, it's no surprise that he fre q uently ranks in the top ten of all dogs registered with the American Kennel Club (AKC).

How is it, then, that a dog who weighs less than a sack of potatoes, has a bony apple head, and spends his time either intimidating intruders or looking for a lap, is so appealing?

It's the cute factor. With this breed it's all about being adorable and affectionate, graceful and alert, swift-moving and compact. And the Chihuahua does it all with a saucy expression that says, "I'm fearless; bite me!"

Here's a breed with presence. Tenacious and tough, you know when a Chihuahua's around because you're no longer in charge. The Chihuahua has no clue that he's smaller than y ou.

There are other reasons for the Chi's star q uality. He needs little grooming, doesn't need much exercise, and once inside your bag, he travels light.

## A Toy Breed

The AKC assigns every breed to one of seven groups: Sporting, Hound, Working, Terriers, Toys, Non-Sporting, and Herding. The Chihuahua belongs to the Toy Group.

All breeds in the Toy Group are small, but beyond that, each one has distinguishing traits that set it apart from other toy breeds.

### What Is a Breed Standard?

A breed standard is a detailed description of the perfect dog of that breed. Breeders use the standard as a guide in their breed- ing programs, and judges use it to evaluate the dogs in confor- mation shows. The standard is written by the national breed club, using guidelines established by the registry that recog- nizes the breed (such as the AKC or UKC).

The first section of the breed standard gives a brief overview of the breed's history. Then it describes the dog's general appearance and size as an adult. Next is a detailed description of the head and neck, then the back and body, and the front and rear legs. The standard then describes the ideal coat and how the dog should be presented in the show ring. It also lists all acceptable colors, patterns, and markings. Then there's a section on how the dog moves, called gait. Finally, there's a general description of the dog's temperament.

Each section also lists characteristics that are considered to be faults or dis q ualifications in the conformation ring. Superficial faults in appearance are often what distinguish a pet- q uality dog from a show- or competition- q uality dog. However, some faults affect the way a dog moves or his overall health. And faults in temperament are serious business.

While car and appliance models change from year to year, breeds remain the same because there is a breed standard. Breeders hope that fifty years from now, a Chihuahua will look very much like the dog you see today.

The standard for the Chihuahua was recorded by the Chihuahua Club of America in 1923. Over the years, there have been changes to the standard, usually for clarification. Even with some slight changes, the Chihuahua has remained a relatively stable breed in physical characteristics and has changed very little since his arrival in the United States.

# The Ideal Chihuahua

Many dogs are intelligent and have wonderful personalities, but it's the Chihuahua's physical appearance that makes him uni q ue. This is a compact breed with a saucy expression and a terrier-like temperament.

## S i ze

Most Chihuahuas are 6 to 9 inches tall when measured from the ground to the top of the shoulders (the withers), and weigh no more than 6 pounds. Some Chihuahuas are larger than that, and although these dogs can't be shown in breed competition, they are wonderful pets and can be much healthier than the very tiny dogs.

Chihuahuas weighing less than 3 pounds are often called "teacups," "pockets," or "tinies," but these are not another variety of the breed. There is only one designated size of Chihuahua. Some people selling puppies will advertise these little ones as exotic and more valuable, but they're actually just the runts of the litter. Teacups have many health problems and very short life spans.

Chihuahuas come in coats of many colors and combinations: all one color, marked (white areas on a colored background), or splashed (irregularly patched color on white or white on color). Just a few of the colors are white, peach, lemon, silver-sand, mole, sable, chocolate, blue, red, tan, and fawn. Don't pay more for a supposedly "rare" color, because there is no such thing!

There are two coat varieties, as well: Smooth and Long Coat. Both have the same breed characteristics. Breeders often have Smooth and Long Coat puppies in the same litter, and both types shed.

## The Smooth

Smooths have a very short coat that lies close to the body. They may have an undercoat—a layer of soft hair under the top, or outer, coat. The coat may be sparser (approaching baldness) on the chest, the temples of the head, and the ears. The tail has furry hair. The Long Coat is soft and full, with fringes along the ears and a ruff around the neck.

The Smooth should also have a slight ruff around his neck, but no fringes or plume like the Long Coat. If the Smooth Chihuahua doesn't have an undercoat, he won't have a full ruff around the neck and won't have a tail that is heavily coated.

Smooth Chihuahuas are more popular than the Long Coats, and many people don't even know that Long Coats exist.

## The Long Coat

Long Coat Chis have a long, soft, double coat that's either flat or slightly curly, about one to one- and-one-half inches long, with a definite undercoat. The long coat has fringe, sometimes called feath- ering, around the edges of the ears; a ruff around the neck; wisps of hair extending along the back of each leg; long hair, called pants, at the buttocks; and long, flowing hair, called a plume, on the tail.

## The Ch i huahua Breed Club

Are you a Chihuahua fan? Want to meet other Chihuahua fanciers? Would you like to Iearn more about Chi behavior, care, and training? If so, contact the Chihuahua Club of America (CCA), a national breed club formed in 1923 under the auspices of the AKC. The CCA is the parent organization of local Chihuahua clubs throughout the United States.

Members of the national breed club wrote the original breed standard of the Chihuahua, under AKC guidelines, and the CCA maintains it. The CCA holds national dog shows, meets regularly, and disburses information about the breed. Since 1987 it has produced five handbooks containing articles about the breed, facts about the club's history, and information about pedigrees.

A Chihuahua owner can apply for membership in the club and join the network of dedicated Chi breeders and owners who care deeply about maintaining the Chihuahua. For further information, contact the Chihuahua Club of America (listed in the appendix).

# Head

This breed's head is his crowning glory and the Chihuahua's most distinguishing characteristic. Chihuahuas have large, well-rounded, "apple dome" skulls. The skull is round like an apple and may have a soft spot, known as a molera, at the top. When you gently rub your hand over the molera, you'll feel a slight inden- tation. More details about the molera are in chapter 8.

The muzzle, sometimes called the snout, is moderately short and slightly pointed. An excessively short muzzle is not desirable because the teeth may become crowded or breathing problems, including frequent snorting, may result.

The nose is very dark in dark-colored dogs and lighter in light-colored dogs.

## Eye s

The Chi's eyes are large, set well apart, radiant, and shiny. They're somewhat full, but not protruding. They should never bulge like the eyes of some of the very short-nosed toy breeds. Although eye color is usually dark, lighter eyes are permissible in light-colored dogs. The ruby eye has a reddish cast to it and is generally found only on very deep red-colored dogs. It's very pretty but is not as common as the dark brown eyes.

## Ears

Another distinguishing feature of the Chihuahua's head is his ears. Chi ears are q uite large and erect and are set somewhat low on the head. When the ears are at rest, they point to about ten o'clock and two o'clock. When alert, they are carried closer to eleven o'clock and one o'clock, or slightly higher. Ears that are carried as high as twelve o'clock are considered too high and make the dog look rabbitlike.

While a puppy is teething, the ears may be up one day and down the next. Ears are usually fully erect between three and six months of age. If the ears are not standing up by eight months of age, they may never become erect. Erect ears or not, you will still have a very nice pet Chihuahua.

## Body

Slightly arched, the Chi's neck slopes gracefully into the shoulders. The body itself is well-balanced. When you measure a Chihuahua from the shoulder to the buttocks, his length is slightly longer than his height. He has a strong, level back, or topline. He also has very dainty feet with well-divided toes. A Chihuahua should look well-balanced and graceful.

# Movement

The Chihuahua moves q uickly with strong, sturdy action. Good structure means a healthy dog who can run and play without any restrictions.

## Temperament

Fearless, tenacious, and terrierlike, the typical Chi temperament is not fearful, q uivering, or cowering. He makes an excellent watchdog, and also likes to enter- tain his family with his singing ability. If he hears a soprano solo, he'll toss his head back and burst into song. At least, that's what he thinks his yodely, whiny sounds are. But a singing Chihuahua won't win a Grammy any time soon.

## The Chihuahua's H is tory

Scientists believe all dog breeds evolved from only one wild ancestor. Contemporary dog breeds were created and domesticated through selec- tive breeding. People bred to obtain the q ualities they desired for certain useful purposes. That's why we have breeds that can track, herd, hunt, guard, and hunt in underground burrows. And that's why there are breeds that are strictly com- panion animals. The Chihuahua is generally classified as a companion dog, pri- marily because of her diminutive size, even though she can be trained to do many useful things.

The Chihuahua's ancestry is so steeped in myth, secondhand stories, and con- troversial history that it is almost impossible to separate fact from fiction. The lit- tle that was recorded in bygone days was written in an archaic form of Spanish, making later interpretation difficult. Several theories of the Chihuahua's origin are presented here because all the fables, legends, and stories are fun to read and discuss, even though they may not be true.

# Mex i can Origins

There are people who insist the Chihuahua is a native Mexican breed because ancient relics of small doglike creatures were found in the archeological remains of the Mayans, the Toltecs, and the Aztecs. The National Museum in Mexico City houses some interesting sculptures. One is of a small dog with large ears, kissing her master. Another sculpture depicts a woman and a child; the woman is carrying a small, erect-eared dog, supposedly a Chihuahua, under one arm. However, Mayan history is very obscure, and some of these early statues bear lit- tle or no resemblance to the modern-day Chihuahua.

# Toltec Civilization

Sketchy information is available about the Toltec culture, which existed around the ninth century in what is now Mexico. Many believe the modern-day Chihuahua is a direct descendant of a dog called the Techichi, depicted in the stone carvings of the monastery of Huejotzingo. The small dogs pictured there bear a more striking resemblance to our present-day Chihuahua.

According to a theory that first appeared in print in 1904, the Techichi was crossed with a wild breed called the Perro Chihuahueno. This breed originally lived in the wild mountains of Chihuahua, where it foraged on anything edible. The dogs supposedly lived in holes in the ground; had round heads, short pointed noses, large erect ears, slender legs, and long toenails; and were wild and untrainable.

# Aztec Culture

The statues from the Aztec era bear an even more striking resemblance to our current dogs. The Aztecs con- quered the Toltecs, and their civiliza- tion flourished for two centuries, from about 1300 to 1520. A small dog was particularly revered by the Aztecs and became the prized posses- sion of the rich. It is said that these little dogs were so treasured by roy- alty that some families had several hundred. The little dogs supposedly led a life of luxury and were pam- pered and cared for by slaves; they were even fed a special diet. During that period, the blue Chihuahua was considered especially sacred. Even today, a blue Chihuahua is unusual.

The little dogs were even buried with their wealthy owners because it was believed that the sins of the interred would be transmitted to the dog, thus ensuring a safe resting place for the master. It was also believed that the little dog would see her master safely along the journey through the underworld, guiding the deceased through all kinds of dangerous places in the afterlife.

# Med i terranean Root s

Some people believe the Chihuahua originated in the Mediterranean region and then became established on the island of Malta. A small dog with the molera trait, found only in the Chihuahua, inhabited that island. From there, the breed was supposed to have been introduced to European countries by sailors in trad- ing ships.

Small dogs resembling Chihuahuas can be found in many paintings by European masters. The most noted work is a fresco painted by Sandro Botticelli, circa 1482, located in the Sistine Chapel. The painting is one of a series depict- ing the life of Moses and clearly shows a small, round-headed, smooth-coated little dog with long nails, large eyes, and large ears that closely resembles a mod- ern-day Chihuahua. Because this painting was done before Columbus arrived in the New World, it leads one to reconsider the theory that the Chihuahua is a native Mexican dog.

### Why Choo s e a Ch i huahua?

Dogs are amazing creatures. Even when you think you know exactly how a dog might react to a certain situation, he'll surprise you. Perhaps it's because dogs lack the verbal skills that people have and rely instead on cues they take from the environment and by paying very close attention to human body language. Dogs notice every little thing you say and do.

They're born with a sort of canine compass, or some very special skills that guide them throughout their life. These have been refined over generations of breeding to sustain and protect them from danger.

Once you know how dogs view the world, you'll be in a better position to decide if you really want to have a dog. Can you live with a dog, and especially a Chihuahua, who is capable of outsmarting you? Think about it.

## Are You Ready?

Are you ready to add a dog to your life? This is a very big decision. The average life span of a Chihuahua is 12 to 17 years, and some have even lived a few years longer. Once you make up your mind to have a dog, he is your responsibility for the rest of his life, regardless of what he does. Your dog will be relying on you to feed, exercise, love, heal, and dress him. Well, clothes are optional, but it's not like he can go out and get a job and hire his own cook, housekeeper, personal trainer, and chauffeur. You are his main s q ueeze.

When you have a dog, it's practically like having a child because it's a commitment of your time, money, and energy. Hopefully, you're not thinking about getting a dog on the spur of the moment. If so, you'll be living with your impulse for a long time. Thousands of dogs are abandoned every year because their owners no longer want the responsibility.

Give this decision a lot of thought and consider how a dog will change your life. First ask yourself how much experience you have with dogs and if you know how to care for one. If you haven't been the one who is totally responsible before, you'll need to spend time learning what to do—which takes time. You'll need to take your dog to training classes, talk to other dog owners, and read books and magazines about dogs.

# T i me, Money, Energy

If you have owned a dog before and know the basics, do you have enough time to spend with a dog now? Don't forget that you are the center of your dog's uni- verse and that he needs your attention and affection. Today, many people work long hours and may not feel like playing with a dog, let alone taking him to a training class or out for a walk, or giving him a bath. Plus, there's the cleanup. The Chihuahua may be small but he's just as capable of making a mess and chewing up your best pair of shoes as a larger dog is.

Can you realistically afford to keep a dog? Will his expenses fit within your budget, and do you really want to allocate your discretionary income to caring for a dog? After you pay the breeder or donate to the rescue organization to ac q uire him, your dog will need bedding, toys, a leash, a collar, grooming tools, and training classes.

If you rent your house or apartment, landlords re q uire extra deposits or cleaning fees if you have a dog. And although a Chihuahua doesn't eat that much, dog food is another expense. Your dog will always need regular veterinary care, plus those middle-of-the-night trips to the emergency clinic, which can be expensive.

What about other family members? Do they want a dog too? If not, there may be disagreements about the dog's care and training, which puts a strain on everyone.

Are there children in your home? If so, you'll always have to supervise your dog when a child is around. You can never predict what either will do, purposely or accidentally, and it's your job to make sure neither is hurt. Will the dog be sharing space with other dogs or animals? If so, there may be issues with every- one getting along.

Certainly, having a dog can be wonderful. Just make sure you're ready and know ahead of time, before you acquire one, what you're getting into. Once you bring a dog home, he's yours for life.

Chihuahuas are very tiny, and that presents a set of challenges that you must be ready to deal with.

# Why a Ch i huahua?

Intelligent and intuitive, today's Chihuahua refuses to be ignored. With confidence to the max, the Chi takes on an intruder or another dog ten times his size without a moment's hesitation. One look at his piercing marble eyes and there's no q uestion that here's a dog who will keep you on your toes. He'll watch your every step and anticipate your next move. If you sit in his favorite spot on the couch, he'll just nap on your lap.

Exercise isn't high on the Chihuahua's priority list, but if you take him for a walk, he'll enjoy it. Training goes q uickly, unless you repeat the lessons too many times. Once he knows what's expected of him, a Chi is bored with repetition unless it's his idea or you praise him for doing it right every time.

Sometimes he enjoys playing with small s q ueaky toys, sometimes not, and children are iffy unless they're well behaved and know how to act around a Lilliputian leader.

Some people are small-dog people and some are not. Which one are you? To have a satisfying relationship with a Chihuahua, it helps to be a small dog lover. This means being able to appreciate the special gifts this size has to offer and to accept the special needs of minis that you'll always have to be aware of. Why then, are you thinking of getting one?

## Chihuahua Character is t i c s

• Affectionate and cuddly

• Lives a long time

• Delicate

• Needs minimal grooming and exercise • Has a shrill, loud bark

• Needs to be kept warm • Needs little space

Space Savers

A Chihuahua is ideal for anyone who enjoys living life on the small side. This breed doesn't take up much space inside your home, and, unlike with a big dog, you won't have to worry about him leaping onto the kitchen counter and steal- ing your sandwich. He won't be jumping up and knocking you over anytime soon. Taking a toy dog for a walk doesn't re q uire a lot of brute strength or ath- letic endurance, either.

Chihuahuas can handle a variety of climates and living q uarters. They adapt well to small homes, but if you live in an apartment or condo, don't assume that you can have pets. In many places dogs aren't allowed, or if they are, the rental agents or co-op board may have strict rules prohibiting dogs from barking and disturbing neighbors. Because the Chihuahua's bark is loud and shrill, this can be a problem, especially if you're late getting home and your dog hears a noise or he's bored.

A dog who weighs less than 5 pounds can s q ueeze through the gate or slip underfoot without your noticing until it's too late. While it's convenient that a Chihuahua doesn't need much room to be happy, too much room can be haz- ardous to his health. If there are too many little nooks and crannies around your property, leave it to a Chihuahua to find them and get stuck where you may not be able to find him so easily.

Many Chihuahuas have suffered broken bones after someone accidentally steps on them. Having a toy dog means learning how to shuffle your feet around when you walk so you don't step on him, and always checking to see where your Chi is before turning around.

## Low-Ma i ntenance

The Chihuahua is considered a nat- ural dog. He doesn't need his tail docked or his ears cropped. His coat doesn't need to be trimmed, stripped, shaved, or plucked. Bathe and brush him, trim his nails, brush his teeth, and clean his eyes and ears, and he's good to go anywhere. Your Chi is a real wash-and-wear model!

Know ahead that Chihuahuas do shed some. The Long Coats blow (lose much of their fur) twice a year, while the Smooths shed all year round.

# A Good Buddy

Chihuahuas can be classified as lap dogs and cuddlers. They enjoy being with you all the time, whether awake or asleep. For every affectionate pat they receive, you'll get double pay- back in love and loyalty.

Chihuahuas like to be massaged and will often roll over for a belly rub. Use caution when massaging a puppy's ears to avoid damaging the ear cartilage, which will prevent the ears from becoming erect.

The Chihuahua is happiest when he is around people, particularly his own- ers. He likes to do what you're doing, especially when it comes to sleeping in your bed, but it's not safe to have him in your bed at night. You might acciden- tally roll over on top of him in the middle of the night.

It's best to train your dog to sleep in his own bed or in a crate. That way, he won't have a chance to steal the covers.

# Along for the R i de

Chihuahuas make wonderful traveling companions because they can accompany you practically anywhere. Riding in an airline-approved crate or carry-on bag, they're allowed under your seat in an airplane and they easily fit in just about any car.

Because they are so easy to care for and don't need a lot of exercise, Chihuahuas make great pets for seniors. Many department stores even let people bring toy dogs with them, but if you're that determined to carry a small dog around with you while shopping, try putting a doggy sweater on a five-pound bag of sugar and carrying that around with you first. It won't take long to realize how sore your arms are! While you can easily drop the bag of sugar off when it gets too heavy, you can't do that with your dog.

## Needs L i ttle Exercise

Compared to a dog of 50-plus pounds, a Chihuahua needs very little exercise. He'll get enough of a cardio workout just running around the house. If this isn't enough, he might enjoy trotting around your backyard, and you can always take him out for a walk.

Chihuahuas love to go for short walks, but be prepared for strangers who want to know more about your tiny trotter. Chihuahuas are fast-moving little dogs who are bred to keep up with their owners while walking, but if your dog gets tired, pick him up and carry him the rest of the way home before he becomes physically exhausted.

If jogging is your thing, don't overdo it with your Chihuahua. A two-mile run may be okay for you, but not for your toy dog. A young Chi has little endurance for running, perhaps only a few yards, and he'll need a regular train- ing regiment and conditioning to run much more than that. An older Chihuahua would be able to trot with you over a greater distance, but certainly not more than half a mile. Remember that a human stride of three feet is q uite a distance for a tiny dog.

## Likes to Play

Playtime with your Chihuahua can be a form of exercise for both of you. A Chihuahua will chase a ball, catch a soft disc, and retrieve small items, but what- ever you use for playtime, be sure that your Chihuahua can't swallow it.

## Come s  in Color s

If you're the kind of person who likes to pick and choose colors, a Chihuahua will fulfill that desire. The breed standard allows Chihuahuas to be any solid color or any combi- nation of colors.

Don't give your dog any stuffed toys that have hard plastic eyes or noses that could fall out and he can swallow, any toys with strings or rib- bons that he could choke on, or toys with internal noisemakers that your dog can rip out and swallow. If the toy can fit easily into the Chihuahua's mouth, it's too small and is poten- tially dangerous for the dog.

Long Lived

You're going to have your Chihuahua for a long time. Their average life span is 12 to 17 years, with some living to 20 years or more! With plenty of q uality medical care, the right food, responsible training, and a loving environment, you'll be able to enjoy a long relationship with your Chihuahua.


# Why Not a Ch i huahua?

A Chihuahua can be a challenge. He's not a passive dog, and not everyone likes a dog who can think for himself and isn't always so willing to please. He has some special needs, too, which have already been mentioned.

## Fam i ly Dog? Maybe

In an all-adult household, a Chihuahua may be the dog of your dreams. A house full of grownups is usually q uiet and orderly, with few loud surprises to startle your Chi. Still, some people complain that a Chihuahua isn't a "man's dog" because of the stereotype that all men like big, rough-and-tumble dogs, while women prefer dogs they can snuggle up to.

But today this is a myth, and Chi fans have come a long way. Chihuahuas have no gender bias, and they will warm up to anyone with a lap. All it takes is a Sunday afternoon, a couch, a big-screen TV, and a football game. Where naps are concerned, Chihuahuas are very good at male bonding and are well known for winning over the men in the household. And once men discover how plucky Chis can be, they're usually hooked on them.

Children are a different story. You would think the tiny Chihuahua would be a perfect fit for a child to hold and cuddle, but that's not always the case. This is a delicate breed who is easily injured, and anyone—adult or child—has to be careful around a Chi. If a toddler loses his balance and accidentally falls on the dog, your dog's back can be broken.

A dog isn't a toy, either. Children don't always know how strong they are, and one hard squeeze will hurt your dog so much that he'll yelp or even bite.

This is why parents must always supervise their children whenever the dog is around and never leave the two alone together. If you have to leave the room, even for a minute, take either the child or the dog with you.

If a child leans over a dog, looks directly into his face at eye level, throws something at him, runs toward him, screams, or grabs him, this is so threatening to a dog that he will act quickly to protect himself. He might growl to warn the child or run away. This should be a clue to your child to leave the dog alone! If the warning is ignored and the dog is cornered, he's likely going to bite. Dog bites are extremely dangerous, often disfiguring or trau- matizing a youngster for life. Although it may seem that a dog bites a child for no reason, to a dog's way of thinking, he had every reason to protect himself.

For their own protection, children must be taught early in life what they can and can't do around a dog, and it's the parents' responsibility to watch their chil- dren to make sure that they follow the rules. On the other hand, well-behaved children who understand how to treat a Chihuahua may be rewarded with a life- long companion. It's up to the parents.

## Ea si ly Ch i lled

Finding a place for your Chihuahua to hang around the house is easy. Chis like to be warm. Most love to lie in front of the window when the sun shines directly through it. A Chi also likes to be near the heater in the winter, although this can dry out his coat. (See chapter 6 for information on how to prevent the coat from drying out.)

The Chihuahua particularly likes to be in his own snuggly bed when the air is too cool. One of the ways your Chihuahua will keep warm is to curl up into a ball and tuck his nose under a leg. This gives the dog a pocket of warm air to inhale that helps keep him warm all over.

Some Chihuahuas shiver and shake, which can usually be attributed to fright or a chill. If it's fright from loud noises, unfamiliar surroundings, or previous abusive treatment, obedience classes may help overcome the shaking by building up the dog's confidence.

Chihuahuas get cold easily, so shaking is more likely from a chill. Long Coats seem to be warmer than the Smooths, but if you live where the winters are cold, put a sweater on your Chihuahua if you will be outside for more than five minutes.

Be careful with your Chi on winter walks. Salt, sand, and chemical ice melters are outdoor winter hazards that will play havoc with your dog's feet, so be sure to wash and wipe the Chihuahua's feet when you get home—especially between the toes. A dog can get frostbite and even lose toes, so take care of him in the cold.

## Snort i ng and Snor i ng

The Chihuahua usually doesn't snore, but occasionally he will. A dog may snore because his muzzle is too short. And sometimes a Chihuahua will snort, which is actually a reverse sneeze. A snort occurs because the dog is so close to the ground that dust gets into his nostrils. To alleviate this problem, make a cup with the palm of your hand and place it gently over your dog's nose without

Chihuahuas are easily chilled, but they don't mind dressing up to stay warm.

# The Dog's Sen s e s

The dog's eyes are designed so that he can see well in relative darkness, has excellent peripheral vision, and is very good at tracking moving objects—all skills that are important to a carni- vore. Dogs also have good depth perception. Those advantages come at a price, though: Dogs are nearsighted and are slow to change the focus of their vision. It's a myth that dogs are color- blind. However, while they can see some (but not all) colors, their eyes were designed to most clearly perceive subtle shades of gray—an advantage when they are hunting in low light.

Dogs have about six times fewer taste buds on their tongue than humans do. They can taste sweet, sour, bitter, and salty tastes, but with so few taste buds it's likely that their sense of taste is not very refined.

A dog's ears can swivel independently, like radar dishes, to pick up sounds and pinpoint their location. Dogs can locate a sound in 6/100 of a second and hear sound four times farther away than we can (which is why there is no reason to yell at your dog). They can also hear sounds at far higher pitches than we can.

In their first few days of life, puppies primarily use their sense of touch to navigate their world. Whiskers on the face, above the eyes, and below the jaws are sensitive enough to detect changes in airflow. Dogs also have touch-sensitive nerve end- ings all over their bodies, including on their paws.

Smell may be a dog's most remarkable sense. Dogs have about 220 million scent receptors in their nose, compared to about 5 million in humans, and a large part of the canine brain is devoted to interpreting scent. Not only can dogs smell scents that are very faint, but they can also accurately distinguish between those scents. In other words, when you smell a pot of spaghetti sauce cooking, your dog probably smells tomatoes and onions and garlic and oregano and whatever else is in the pot.

## Good Watchdog s

Chihuahuas are excellent watchdogs. Their hearing is acute and their bark is loud and shrill. They have been known to scare burglars and warn owners of fire and other dangers. Because the dog's hearing is so sharp, a Chihuahua will alert the family before anyone in the household is aware of impending disaster. One owner claims that his Chihuahua has always warned him of snakes in his back- yard! Another Chihuahua alerted his owner to an intruder entering the house in the middle of the night. The burglar didn't stay long, because the loud and con- stant barking was a deterrent.

Chihuahuas don't bark any more than many other breeds, and they can be trained to be quiet on command. If you want your dog to protect you, allow him to bark when strangers approach or at unusual situations. But you should discourage excessive and constant barking for no reason.

Chihuahuas won't run up to a visiting houseguest and jump all over the per- son. They are cautious about accepting a stranger and may continue to bark until you tell them to be q uiet. Your Chihuahua will not be aggressive but will look over the guest from a distance, approaching with caution before deciding all is well. The guest should allow the Chihuahua to take the initiative and make the first friendly overtures; this will put the dog more at ease. This doesn't mean your dog is shy—just aware that someone who is not a member of the family is in the house.

With a dog as small as a Chihuahua, the guest shouldn't bend over the dog because the dog may interpret this as a menacing move. Instead, the person should try s q uatting next to the dog. The next step is to try petting the Chihuahua's chest, neck, shoulder, or back, which is less menacing than reach- ing for the top of the head.

This cautious awareness of sur- roundings and people may be due to the Chihuahua's diminutive size. If the dog were to eagerly run up to a guest, the person could scoop up the dog quickly, perhaps dropping or injuring him in some way. If a Chihuahua eagerly accepted strangers, he wouldn't be much of a watchdog, either.

## Ch i huahua s  and Other Dogs

Chihuahuas usually get along well with other breeds, but when a small dog is first introduced into a household that already has a dog, both must be carefully supervised until you're certain they are getting along well.

Many Chihuahua owners have more than one. Two dogs mean more care and training but, in general, double the enjoyment. Also, the two Chihuahuas make good playmates for each other. If you're adding a second dog, choose one of the opposite sex because they will get along better, but they must be spayed and neutered. With multiple dogs, one is always the "top dog" because he's in charge of the other. If two or more Chihuahuas are in residence, each will develop his own distinct personality.

Chihuahuas can get along well with other dogs, but supervise carefully when you first introduce them.

## Choo si ng Your Chihuahua

If you can't decide whether you want a puppy or an older Chihuahua, just think about choosing chocolate or vanilla. Both ages and flavors are yummy, and each one has advantages and disadvantages. Regardless of which one you choose, your new little Miss Chi will be with you for 12 to 17 years, so learn as much as you can about the behavior, care, and training of puppies and adult dogs before you pick one. Raising a dog is a lifetime commitment, and you want to be sure you can handle it.

Once you decide on either a puppy or an adult and know you can devote what it takes to care for her, the next step is finding the best breeder or a good rescue or shelter organization. Make the right choice now and you'll discover later on that adding a Chihuahua to your household was the best decision you ever made. Maybe you'll even decide to add a second Chi from another source. No one says you have to pick chocolate every time.

# All Your Cho i ce s

To decide if you want a puppy or an adult Chi, consider how much dog experi- ence, patience, time, and money you have. Each age has different needs that you may or may not want to provide. That's okay. Once you know what those needs are, you can choose the canine companion you really want instead of just taking the first adorable Chi who comes your way.

Once the age question is settled, don't relax just yet. You still have to decide if you want a male or a female, a Smooth or a Long Coat, and the color you pre- fer (if you have a preference).

## Puppy Love

Think you want a puppy? Who doesn't love seeing a cute puppy and all the funny things she does? Probably the person who has to get up in the middle of the night to take her outside to go potty or tell someone that their best pair of leather shoes now has tiny teeth marks. Of course, one little kiss from a Chi baby and all is forgiven—until she needs more attention.

Besides housetraining, crate training, and all the other kinds of training a Chi puppy needs, there's keeping an eye on her 24/7 and a feeding schedule to maintain. Toy puppies must have a meal several times a day for the first few months, plus some exercise and regular outings for socialization. Raising a puppy can be a full-time job, and not everyone is up to the challenge. Plus, it's expensive.

Be prepared to pay several hundred dollars to buy a quality puppy from a reputable breeder. You may think the initial cost of a Chihuahua puppy is expensive, but it's sometimes a lot less than what you'll have to spend on pet supplies.

Puppies certainly have their charms, but they can get into a lot of trouble. Chihuahuas live a long time, and adult dogs can make great pets.

During her first year of life, your Chihuahua puppy will also need to visit the veterinarian a few times for vaccinations (see chapter 8 for more on that). Will you be able to leave work early to take her, and will the cost of these visits fit into your budget? And what about all those supplies you have to buy for her, such as a crate, dog dishes, grooming accessories, shampoo, training classes, a collar, a leash, microchipping, puppy food, and toys? Can you afford these?

Some people prefer having a puppy because they want to do all the training and socializing themselves. They want to build a bond with their dog as early as possible and know that she has a solid start. Or they want to meet the breeder, see their puppy's sire and dam, and the conditions the puppy was raised in, and watch her grow into adulthood.

If you can take all the pros and cons of having a young Chi in stride, then a puppy is definitely the right choice for you.

# An Adult Ch i

What about an adult Chihuahua? A puppy becomes an adult on her first birth-day, so if you choose to ac q uire an adult Chi she may still be a youngster. Generally though, re-homed Chihuahuas are 4 years old and up.

Whatever her adult age, an older Chi may not be housetrained and may take a little longer to warm up to you. She may also have a few bad habits and you'll have to spend some time retraining her. Plus, you might not know anything about where she originally came from or how she spent her early years.

Many Chihuahuas are abandoned every year for no reason. Others are given up because they have a behavior problem and the owner doesn't want to spend the time or energy to properly train the dog to be a good member of the household.

Happily, there are many older dogs who make great pets and can give you many years of companionship. An older Chi won't need constant supervision and will only require two meals a day, which is an easier schedule to manage. Some older Chi girls may already be housetrained and have good manners. If not, you can always teach an old dog new tricks! Most older dogs have lost inter- est in chewing things up and are just happy curling up on your lap or going for a short walk, so you don't have to worry about what your dog is doing all the time.

Chances are you won't have to pay very much to adopt an older dog, either. Shelters and rescue organizations usually re q uest a minimal fee or donation, and sometimes the dog is even free.

Perhaps the best part about ac q uiring an older dog is that you are giving her a home and saving her life.

A pink or a blue Chi collar? Surely you'll be happy with either sex. Both are sweet and loving, although there are a few differences. The males tend to be more even-tempered, but show no shame about licking their private parts in public or mounting your leg, a guest's leg, or even a throw pillow. They mount to show dominance and may mark their territory by lifting their legs and uri- nating on anything in or out of the house.

To control your male's enthusiasm, take him to obedience class and establish who's in charge. Watching him closely in the house may prevent him from water- ing the edge of your couch, but neutering usually stops these bad boy habits.

While some Chi girls will mount, too, if they're dominant, this usually stops once they've been spayed. If a dog isn't spayed it's a hassle. Every five to seven months she'll come in season and have a messy, bloody discharge that lasts for three weeks. She'll do whatever it takes to find a male, even if it means escaping out the front door. The females tend to be moodier than the males and more protective of the house, too.

## Smooth or Long Coat?

There are a few differences between the two that you should consider.

Smooths seem to be more popular than Long Coats, although that may be because many people aren't aware that longhaired Chis even exist. Many breeders say the

When choosing between the two coat types, think about how much you mind having dog hair around the house.

Smooths are more outgoing and not as reserved as the Long Coats, and that Smooths are cuddlier. Chihuahuas with long coats often prefer to sit next to you rather than in your lap and can tolerate the cold a little more than the short- haired dogs, who shiver when it even looks chilly.

When choosing between the two coat types, think about how you like to clean up dog hair: big clumps all at once, or a few tiny hairs sticking into your clothes and furniture all the time? Long Coats blow their coats (lose a lot of hair quickly) twice a year, while the Smooths shed a little all year long.

You've probably seen more fawn-colored Chihuahuas than any other color, because they are the most popular. Both Smooths and Long Coats come in all different color combinations, and all are acceptable in the show ring, but there is no such thing as a rare-colored Chihuahua. If someone wants to sell you a rare Chi for a lot of money, don't be taken in. No Chi color is rare.

Chihuahuas can be solid (all one color), marked (white areas on a colored background), or splashed (irregularly patched color on white or white on color). Some of the solid colors you'll see are peach, lemon, silver-sand, mole, sable, chocolate, blue, red, tan, and fawn.

Chis can also have spots or two colors, such as white and gold or chocolate and white. Some reputable breeders may prefer to breed for a certain color or pattern, but many have Chihuahuas in all colors. Whatever color you see on the outside, know that all Chihuahuas are the same little saucy dogs on the inside.


# F i nd i ng a Puppy

Now that you know you want a puppy and what sex, coat type, and color are your first choices, your next decision is where to look for the Chi of your dreams. Chihuahuas are so popular that you'll see puppies just about everywhere you look: breeders, the Internet, advertisements, pet stores, shelters, and even in a box in front of the supermarket. You may wonder if there's any difference among these. Aren't all Chihuahua puppies the same, no matter where you find them? Hardly! Here are the differences.

## Responsible Breeder s

Anyone can call themselves a breeder, but not all breeders are created e q ual. If you're looking for a healthy, even-tempered pet Chihuahua, the best place to go is the home of a responsible breeder.

This person is breeding dogs for the show ring. The breeder is usually a member of the Chihuahua Club of America, a regional Chihuahua club, and maybe a local kennel club. The breeder has dedicated many years to knowing everything about the behavior, care, health, and training of Chihuahuas and gives a lot of thought to selecting a q uality sire and dam for every litter bred.

The breeder's goal isn't to sell every puppy in the litter as an extra income. Many responsible breeders even lose money when they breed a litter because they spare no expense in taking care of the mother and all her puppies. The rea- son they breed is because they want to maintain the q uality and health of the breed for future generations. To prove their stock, they exhibit their dogs at AKC dog shows and breed only the best dogs they have.

Going to a responsible show breeder doesn't mean you'll have to buy a show puppy, but that's where the best pet- q uality pups will be. Not every puppy in a litter has the conformation or personality to be a show dog, but all the pups in the litter were bred and raised the same way as the top show prospects.

In quality litters like this, one or both of the parents are usually AKC champions and the breeder has tested them and knows they are free from any genetic weaknesses they could pass on to their offspring.

At the breeder's home, you'll be able to see the conditions the pups are raised in, the mother and perhaps the father (or a picture of him), and other relatives such as the puppies' grandparents, aunts or uncles, or half-brothers and sisters.

Responsible breeders prove the quality of their dogs by competing with them. The puppy you get from a breeder will be healthy and ready to face the world.

Observe these relatives; their appearance and behavior will tell you what your Chi puppy will grow up to look and act like.

Before selling any puppy, the breeder screens buyers and chooses the best ones. The breeder has worked too hard breeding the best to just sell them to someone who might not care for them in the long run. Be prepared to discuss your prior experience with a toy dog, how you will train or socialize your Chi, where the dog will be kept, if your yard is secure, and if there are children at home.

No responsible breeder sells puppies to a broker or to a pet store, because the breeder has no way of knowing who the new owners will be or if they can prop- erly care for the puppy forever. The breeder feels permanently responsible for every dog bred and will gladly take a dog back if the owner can't take care of her.

When you go to a responsible breeder you're just not buying a puppy. You're also buying the breeder's expertise. The breeder will answer any q uestions you ever have about your Chihuahua.

How do you find responsible breeders? The AKC and the Chihuahua Club of America have a network of breeders they can refer you to. Also check with a local kennel club, your veterinarian, and other Chihuahua owners for breeders they recommend.

Chihuahua litters are very small, averaging one to three puppies, so it may be a little difficult to find a puppy. But Chihuahua breeders are always in touch with one another, even cross-country, so someone will know where to find puppies.

## Backyard Breeder

Although you'll probably pay less for a backyard-bred puppy, this breeder is breeding for all the wrong reasons. The person may breed a litter because they want to make extra money or so the kids can see a birth. They haven't studied the breed in detail, have no long-term commitment to the future of the breed, and may not have done any health tests on their dogs, so they don't know what genetic diseases their dogs might be passing on to the puppies.

They don't know about pedigrees and will thus breed any male to any female Chihuahua, regardless of their temperament or appearance. One parent may not even be a Chihuahua, may not be AKC-registered, or may hardly resemble what a Chihuahua is supposed to look and act like.

These breeders do not show their dogs, so they're not proving their stock in the show ring and have no incentive to produce the best q uality Chihuahuas they possibly can. They don't screen their buyers, either. Anyone with enough money can buy a puppy from a backyard breeder.

Backyard breeders may say they raise their puppies in their own home and treat them like their own children, but let's face it: If someone always has litters year round, how much personal one-on-one time do they really have available to spend with them? Puppies fail to thrive if they're not handled a lot and intro- duced to many different sights and sounds during their first few weeks of life. These are the Chihuahuas who grow up to be frightened or overly aggressive, and whose owners give up and abandon them years later.


The Internet

Go online to find a puppy and you'll see hundreds of Web sites listing Chihuahua pups for sale. This includes the Chihuahua Club of America, many regional Chihuahua clubs, and responsible show breeders who also offer breed information and have a breeder referral network.

There are many other Web sites owned by puppy brokers and backyard breeders that are very slick and have pictures of puppies available practically year round. How do you tell the difference between the Web sites of responsible show breeders, brokers and commercial breeders, and backyard breeders?

Most commercial and backyard breeders have several different breeds avail-able, and once you give them your credit card number they'll happily ship you a puppy. No q uestions asked and no health guarantees, either. They may send you a pedigree, but you have no way of knowing who the dogs are that are listed. Often the stock isn't AKC-registered, so you can't prove who the sire really is (the AKC re q uires all males who sire more than a few litters to be DNA-tested for proof of identity). This is important if a genetic health problem ever turns up in your dog.

If you find a breeder on the Internet who interests you, call and ask them if their dogs are champions and if so, if you can visit their kennel. Buyer beware!

# CHAPTER TWO

## BREEDING CHIHUAHUAS

Breeding Chihuahuas is defined as planning and organizing the mating of two purebred Chihuahua dogs in order to produce a litter of chihuahua puppies respecting the clear guidelines as set by the official breed standard.

The truth is, Chihuahua breeding should always offer clear or subtle improvement from the previous generation. A Chihuahua breeder doesn't just breed for the sake of breeding or profiting, he or she must breed with clear short and long-term measurable objectives.

The chihuahua isn't the easiest breed to work with. They are small dogs prone to several health issues, but they are indeed very much sought after which makes the breed very appealing for a passionate breeder. In this article, I want to share with you pointers about how to breed chihuahuas of the highest quality without compromising on the breed's common health conditions.

## H is tory of Ch i huahua Breed i ng

For decades, the Chihuahua breed was thought to have originated in China, or at least developed using external blood from miniature dogs of Chinese descent. A recent research paper by The Royal Society B studied the DNA and genetic materials of ancestral American breeds along with some current Latin breeds (e.g. Chihuahua, Peruvian hairless dog, etc.)

Discoveries were clear: the modern Chihuahua shares a lot of genetic material with ancestral breeds from the Americas confirming its indigenous roots. "Our results confirm that American dogs are a remaining part of the indigenous American culture, which underscores the importance of preserving these populations." the study confirmed.

The modern Chihuahua is descending from the Techichi, the favorite dog breed of the Toltec civilization of Mexico. Just like most very ancient dog breeds, the Techichi was a broad type of dog without any official standard. Therefore, you may find two pictures of Techichi dogs that differ very much even if both dogs are labeled the same.

On the timeline, the Techichis was formally traced back from the 9th century but pottery art from Colima, Mexico is vaguely depicting animals looking very similar to Techichi dogs back in 300 BC.

Dogs approximating the modern Chihuahua breed were then found in old materials from the pre-Mayan era, precisely in the Great Pyramid of Cholula. Perhaps due to its peculiar and very appealing look, many memorabilia or drawings of Chihuahua-like dogs have been found over the centuries in obviously Mexico, but also El Salvador, Tennessee, and the surrounding areas. All of which date from 1100 AD onwards.

Sadly, a letter from the Spanish con q uistador Hernan Cortés dated from 1520 explains that these small Chihuahua dogs are being bred, raised and sold as foods. The letter, still available on Fordham University's website, reads "There are also sold rabbits, hares, deer, and little dogs [i.e., the chihuahua], which are raised for eating." The breed wasn't used for any particular purpose or job, besides being a great companion dog. Small dogs like chihuahuas and techichis were thought to absorb pain and sins from humans and were allegedly buried alive with the deads, or used at live water bottles.

The first recorded mentions of a Chihuahua breed date back to 1884 when Mexican traders were breeding Chihuahuas to sell them to tourists in bordering markets. Up until the 20th century and the official recognition of the breed by the American Kennel Club in 1904, the Chihuahua was a dog with many different appearances but always characterized by its tiny size.

## Health Concern s  When Breeding Ch i huahua s

The Chihuahua breed is notoriously small in size and extremely fragile, especially since the breed is also known to be a very excitable and active one. The risk of injuries is higher than the average dog, and puppies will inevitably require a lot of extra care and attention during their handling.

When breeding Chihuahuas, the main goals is to reduce the various health risks by carefully screening each member of your breeding stock, internal and external. The entire breed counts on each of you, Chihuahua breeders, to breed out the below common health concerns before they cannibalize the breed and it's too late (ideally, the Chihuahua doesn't want to be the new English Bulldog.)


Hydrocephalus

Common to most toy breeds, hydrocephalus is the accumulation of too much cerebrospinal fluid in the dog's brain. It's generally visible due to the oversized head of the puppy, showing both an abnormal shape and size. Chihuahuas affected by hydrocephalus are often growing at a much slower rate than the other whelps, and tend to show signs of weakness and lethargy.

Because of the excess fluid within the dog's skull, there is too strong pressure on the brain, the eyes, and the blood supply too. Chances of survival, in the long run, are rather slim, even with early veterinary attention. The solution here is to stop trying to breed to smallest Chihuahua puppies ever and focus on health rather than eye-catching appearances and Facebook likes.


Jaw & Dental Care

Because the chihuahua is such a tiny breed of dogs, their head doesn't have much room for a strong jaw and dentition. Therefore, veterinarians tend to give extra care and run extra checks on Chihuahuas' dental health. From X-rays to regular cleaning, breeders of Chihuahuas should always avoid breeding to smaller sizes in order to avoid huge complications. Periodontal health includes the regular use of dental sticks, but also the inevitable brushing of your dog's teeth. Monitor the gums of a dog is also important.

Molera (Soft Spot)

Specific to the Chihuahua breed, a molera is a soft spot in the dog's skull. It is the Chihuahua's version of what a fontanelle is for human babies. A molera is not a disease, nor it is a defect. Soft spots generally fill themselves up with age but require a lot of attention because it is most definitely a very fragile part of the affected puppy.

At birth, the cartilage and bones forming the dog's skull are softer anyway. But as a normal dog matures, both will strengthen and harden. Chihuahuas affected by a molera, or soft spot, will have a round or diamond-shaped softer spot that will normally remain fragile for several months until it fills itself up.

In 1989, a study paper written by Greene and Braund stated that there is no increased risk of hydrocephalus when a molera is present on the Chihuahua's head: "Many clinically normal toy breeds and brachycephalic (short-faced) breeds also may have open fontanelles without associated hydrocephalus."


Chihuahua Breeding's Best Practices

Although all dog breeds belong to the Canis lupus familiaris species, each particular breed of dogs has its own specificities a breeder must know before getting involved with a breeding program. The Chihuahua is a very popular dog breed and therefore re q uires a lot of care and knowledge.

There are numerous Chihuahuas matingsorganized daily so every (life-threatening) defect could and does spread like the plague, extremely fast. It is your duty to follow the best practices when breeding Chihuahuas in order to take the best dogs you can find today, and improve them tomorrow.

Apple-head Chihuahuas and Deer-head Chihuahuas

Although they belong to the same breed, there are two distinct body and head types within the Chihuahua breed:

• Deer-head Chihuahuas (older type) — the body has larger ears, and longer, more slender legs; flat-topped heads with more widely set eyes.

• Apple-head Chihuahuas (current standard) — a 90° angle where the dog's muzzle joins the forehead, much-rounded heads, close-set eyes, and relatively short ears and legs.

Scientifically, the genetic reasons why these two types coexist are still unknown, but old depictions found in Central America centuries ago lead us to believe that this difference in appearances has perhaps always been there. As explained earlier in the article, the Techichi, ancestor of the Chihuahua, was a type of dog and probably some of them had deer-shaped heads, while others had apple-shaped skulls. Some breed fanciers have also hypothesized that the deer head Chihuahua could come from a cross between the ancestral Techichi and the Chinese Crested.

As a modern breeder, you do want to focus on breeding Apple-head chihuahuas since this is the type currently promoted and recognized by both the American Kennel Club and the Chihuahua Club of America.

There is a small controversy within the Chihuahua circles about Deer Head Chihuahuas and their current dissension by the official breed standards; many believe that deer head chihuahuas should be accepted since they are clearly part of the breed and still very common to this day. Things are not black and white and because of centuries of genetic intermingling, most Chihuahuas bred by hobby breeders will display characteristics from both types, apple and deer head chihuahuas. The triage is mainly performed in dog shows and pet exhibitions.

Smooth vs Long-Hair Chihuahuas

According to the respected and official American Kennel Club, there are two subtypes of Chihuahuas accepted:

• Smooth-Coat Chihuahuas showcasing a very short coat

• Long-Hair Chihuahuas boasting a longer coat all over their body

Both Chihuahua types are genetically identical with their only difference being the length of their coat — there is no best type here, just a matter of preference, with trends favoring one over the other in cycles! Either type generally requires pet clothing during cold days.

Obviously, just like with dog with longer hairs, grooming is re q uired mainly by brushing in order to keep the coat free of tangled hair. Detangling a matted coat is a hassle that often leads long-hair Chihuahua owners to the professional groomer for a quick clip of the dog's coat. If you are experienced yourself, you may want to clean up your Chihuahua's rear-end area by trimming the hair so to avoid the dog soiling its own fur. "The long-coat variety tends to soft and semi-fluffy coat of hair, and they may or may not have an undercoat," said Chihuahua Wardrobe.

## When s hould ch i huahua s breed?

The Chihuahua breed, like other small and toy dogs, tend to sexually mature earlier than larger dogs; generally around 6 months of age. Just like any other dog breed, female Chihuahuas should never be bred on their first two or three heats because fertility is not high enough to allow for a successful and smooth pregnancy.

The back-to-back breeding of smaller dogs (e.g. Chihuahua, Pomeranians, etc) is not recommended because the body and overall support system is not strong enough to cope with repeated pregnancies. Instead, you do want to skip a heat to allow your Chihuahua female a good amount of recovery.

Male Chihuahuas should be used for stud services once they are fully matured, generally after a year or two of age. You also want to wait for the stud to completely grow to assess whether or not it is a good enough specimen to use for future breedings.

## What' s the average l i tter si ze of Chihuahuas?

The average size of a litter of Chihuahua puppies is anywhere between one and three whelps. Four puppies and over is definitely realistic but rare.

If you are wondering how many puppies can a chihuahua have, you need to understand that with canines, the size of a litter is influenced by multiple factors: fertility of the female, size of the female, q uality of the male's semen, diet, current health, etc.

Do Chihuahuas need C-section during the delivery of puppies?

Although the newborn puppies are very small, cesarean sections (i.e. C-sections) are somewhat common for the Chihuahua breed. This is due to the tiny size of the mother's opening. Additionally, the very small uterus of the mother Chihuahua can cause obstructions during the delivery calling for an emergency C-section.

As a responsible dog breeder, you must absolutely have the budget ready in case of urgent C-section, as well as call up your vet few days ahead to make sure they are ready to provide such surgical operation if need be. In most cases, especially with a small puppy count expected at delivery, a natural birth will seamlessly occur; but the breeder's job is to prepare for abnormal situations.

## How much s hould I s ell a purebred Chihuahua puppy for?

The price of each puppy depends on the puppy itself (markings, shape), the pedigree analysis, your reputation, your results in dog shows, the demand in your neighborhood, the current market price, the defects your dogs are showing, etc.

We've written an entire article on how much you should sell your puppies for, and there is no magic number I could give you right here, right now. Remember, there is no rule that says female dogs should have a higher price tag or the opposite with males being pricier than their counterparts.

Is it worth breeding teacup Chihuahuas?

Such "chihuahuas" are flirting with death at each litter and should never be tolerated. If you are wondering how to breed teacup Chihuahuas, you've landed on the wrong page. Unfortunately, the race to breeding the cutest and tiniest dog is encouraged on social media and creates a demand that many breeders are happy to supply for.

The Chihuahua breed, as is, is very small and inherently shows size-specific health problems. Trying to breed smaller and smaller using selective breeding is pure idiocy. I would recommend you to stick to the actual breed standard and not try to jump on a bandwagon that will soon die down when its inherent cruelty is exposed.

Future of the Chihuahua Breed

When poring over how to breeding Chihuahuas, one should mainly focus on the present and future. Indeed, the present means acknowledging the current state of the breed and the bloodlines you have at hand. The future of the breed is where your ambition should lead you towards.

Finally, there is also a huge trend towards crossing Chihuahuas with other small and toy breeds to obtain obscenely cute small hybrid dogs (e.g. the Pomchi).

# Breed i ng Considerations and Risks

Adrienne is a certified dog trainer, behavior consultant, former veterinarian assistant, and author of Brain Training for Dogs.

While it is generally easy to determine when an average dog is in heat, Chihuahua owners may face some extra challenges due to this breed's almost obsessive cleanliness. This means that some Chihuahua dog owners may actually miss their Chihuahua's first heat cycle simply because Chihuahuas are fastidiously clean and will lick away any proof of being in heat, explains Caroline Coile, author of The Chihuahua Handbook.

But when do Chihuahuas go into heat exactly? The time they go into heat really varies from one Chihuahua to another. Most likely, however, the first heat will occur any time between the age of six and eight months on average. There are always exceptions, and a Chihuahua going into heat at five months or at one year old is not unheard of. However, being a small breed makes Chihuahuas go into heat much earlier when compared to much larger dog breeds.

Signs Your Chihuahua Is in Heat

Now that you know when Chihuahuas go into heat, you may be wondering how to recognize the signs suggesting it. The Chihuahua's heat cycle duration averages 21 days and includes the proestrus, estrus, and diestrus. The anestrus is basically a mostly inactive rest period. The cycle can be divided into four precise stages, each e q uipped with distinct features listed below.

Proestrus

This phase lasts anywhere between four to nine days. During this time, your Chihuahua's reproductive tissues may appear puffier than normal. The most evident sign is vaginal bleeding, however, as mentioned earlier, you may barely notice this if you own an overly clean Chihuahua that will lick away any evidence. Male dogs will be q uite interested in your Chihuahua, but she will not allow them to mate as of yet.

Estrus

This phase lasts anywhere between four to thirteen days. The bloody discharge observed in the previous stage will fade out and be replaced by a pink or straw-colored discharge. During this phase, your Chihuahua is officially in "standing heat" which means she will stand still with the tail pulled to the side, allowing the male to mount. This is the phase when she is at the peak of her fertility.

Diestrus

Also known as metestrus, this phase basically concludes the active part of the heat cycle and lasts from 60–90 days. Your Chihuahua will no longer be interested in males, even tough some males may initially still stick around. If your Chihuahua is pregnant, this phase lasts until the birth of puppies, 63 days or so later. If your Chihuahua is not pregnant, diestrus may last two to three months, and during this time dogs may experience a false pregnancy.

Anestrus

Anestrus is simply the phase during which the reproductive organs get to rest. It typically lasts between two and three months. While this sounds much like an inactive q uiet time, in reality, your Chihuahua's pituitary glands and ovaries are getting ready for the next proestrus phase, several months ahead. Consider that Chihuahuas generally go in heat once every five to eight months, so this means your Chihuahua will most likely go in heat twice a year.

Learning when Chihuahuas go into heat is fundamental for any average dog owner or prospective breeder. If you are a dog owner, you must secure your Chihuahua and keep her safely away from intact males. If you are planning on breeding your Chihuahua, you must determine the best time to breed in order to heighten the chances of pregnancy. However, it is imperative to research and learn to be a reputable Chihuahua breeder after reading the important considerations pertaining to breeding Chihuahuas.

How to Care for a Chihuahua in Heat

Upon recognizing the signs of heat, you must do what you can to protect your Chihuahua from the attention of males if you are not planning on breeding. If you are still having a hard time deciphering the potential signs of heat, rest assured, the behavior of intact male dogs will let you know. Do not be surprised if male dogs will show up on your doorstep. According to the American Kennel Club, a male dog is capable of detecting the scent of a dog in estrus up to five miles away!

As a responsible dog owner, you must do as much as you can to keep your Chihuahua away from males. Avoid the dog park, and if you must take her out, have her leashed at all times. Never underestimate the persistence and determination of intact male dogs. They can be q uite creative and use astute planning to dig under or even climb over a fence to get to her. Also, watch the door: even though escaping has never crossed your Chihuahua's mind, when in heat, roaming is more than a mere possibility.

Preventing your Chihuahua from urinating all over the place will also keep males at bay since females urinate q uite fre q uently during their heat cycle simply to leave "calling cards" denoting their availability. The urination may not be isolated to the indoors; in fact, some female dogs will have no problem urinating in the home. And just in case you were wondering about how to protect your furniture and carpet from that bloody discharge, you can invest in a pair of britches, special panties for dogs in heat.

If all the above sounds like too much work, consider spaying your Chihuahua. Spaying is behaviorally and medically beneficial for your dog in many ways, and will solve the problem of unwanted puppies, reducing the enormous burden of pet overpopulation. The ASPCA claims that millions of healthy dogs and cats are put to death each year in the United States just because there are not enough homes for them.

# CONCLUSION

When do chihuahuas go into heat? The answer to this q uestion is particularly important if you are planning to breed your Chihuahua, therefore you must do your homework well to heighten the chances of getting her pregnant. Whether you are planning to breed her naturally, or resort to artificial insemination, you need to figure out the days she is most fertile.

In natural breedings, male dogs simply know when the right time is, and females will stand for them. Generally, this happens between the 8th and the 15th day of heat counting from the day your Chihuahua started bleeding, explains veterinarian Margareth V. Root Kustritz with the University of Minnesota. There are really no guarantees that mating in these days will result in puppies. However, breeders have found that allowing breeding every other day starting from the 7th day of heat up until the female allows it, heightens the chances of success.

If you are artificially inseminating and need to figure out the most fertile days, your veterinarian may help by assessing cells collected from a vaginal swab or by measuring the levels of progesterone in the blood. Ideally, the artificial insemination should be performed twice, two and four days after ovulation, further explains Margareth V. Root Kustritz.

Regardless, of how you intend to mate your dog, breeding is a serious choice, especially when it comes to a breed such as a Chihuahua which has a far more risky pregnancy compared to other larger breeds, explains Marli Medinnus, a professional breeder of AKC Longcoat Chihuahuas in San Jose, California.

Chihuahuas should never be bred on their first heat. They are too young and giving birth may lead to complications. They should be bred instead for the first time during their second or third heat, and before turning three years old. Your Chihuahua should also have the right conformation with a wide pelvic area and a good tuck up in order to heighten the chances of carrying and delivering the pups safely.

Breeding is something that re q uires a lot of expertise with a good amount of knowledge about genetics and ultimate goals about improving the breed in mind. Costs must also be evaluated, since Chihuahuas are prone to requiring Cesarean sections, not to mention expenses associated with testing breeding stock for heritable defects and genetic diseases.

Shots, x-rays, puppy shots, and other unexpected medical treatments are more expenses that must be added to the list. But there is much more than that. If this sounds like a lot of work, your best bet is to spay your Chihuahua and allow her to live her life to the fullest since breeding can also considerably shorten her expected life span.

www.ingramcontent.com/pod-product-compliance
Lightning Source LLC
Chambersburg PA
CBHW020347180726
47991CB00021B/3012